RABBIT

Words that look like **this** can be found in the glossary on page 24.

BookLife
PUBLISHING

©2019
BookLife Publishing Ltd.
King's Lynn
Norfolk PE30 4LS

All rights reserved.
Printed in Malaysia.

A catalogue record for this book is available from the British Library.

ISBN: 978-1-78637-731-9

Written by:
Shalini Vallepur

Edited by:
Emilie Dufresne

Designed by:
Danielle Jones

CONTENTS

WHAT IS A LIFE CYCLE?

All animals, plants and humans go through different stages of their life as they grow and change. This is called a life cycle.

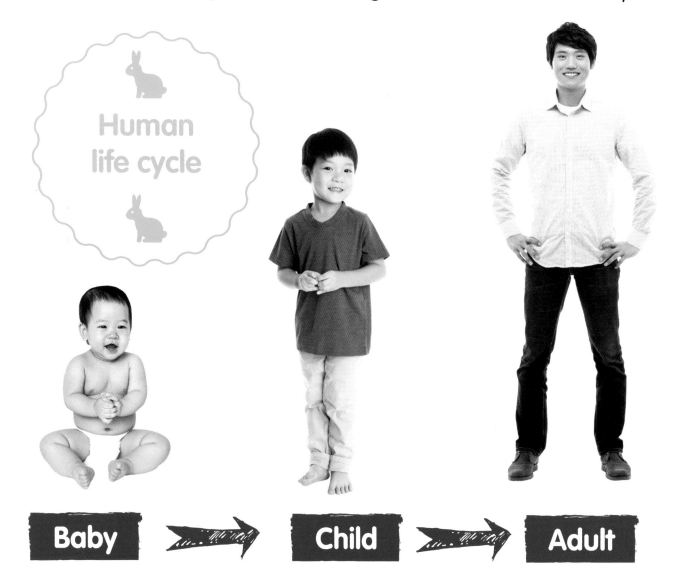

Human life cycle

Baby ➤ **Child** ➤ **Adult**

4

WHAT IS A RABBIT?

A rabbit is a **species** of **mammal**. In the wild, rabbits make their homes underground in **burrows**. They can live in large groups called colonies.

Rabbits have strong legs for hopping.

KITTENS

Baby rabbits are called kittens or kits. Female rabbits are usually **pregnant** for about 30 days and give birth to around six kittens at a time.

A group of kittens is called a litter.

Most kittens are born in a nest inside the burrow. They are born without fur and they can't see or hear anything.

The mother uses grass and pieces of her own fur to make the nest warm.

CHANGING KITTENS

When a kitten is around ten days old, its eyes will open and its ears will stand up. The kittens can now see and hear.

The kittens start to grow lots of fluffy fur!

The kittens stay inside the burrow because they still need to drink their mother's milk. This helps them to grow very quickly.

LIFE IN THE BURROW

Female rabbits often tunnel in the ground to build a burrow. The burrow hides the kittens from **predators** and helps to keep them safe.

Time to
go home!

Kittens live in the burrow with the rest of the colony. There can be up to 30 rabbits living together in burrows connected by tunnels.

All of these connected tunnels are called a warren.

Colony of rabbits

LEAVING THE BURROW

When the kittens are 18 days old, they begin to look outside the burrow. They might go inside other burrows to play with other litters of kittens.

These kittens are peering outside their burrow!

Rabbits are **herbivores** that eat grass, small flowers and leafy plants.

The kittens are **weaned** off their mother's milk when they are around 25 days old. They leave the burrow and drink water and eat plants.

RABBITS

Female kittens become adults when they are three and a half months old. They build their own burrows and nests ready for a new litter.

A female rabbit is called a doe.

Male kittens become adults when they are four months old. They try to find a **mate** of their own.

A male rabbit is called a buck.

TYPES OF RABBIT

Rabbits are common all over the world. There are many different **breeds** of rabbit and they come in different colours and sizes.

Angora rabbit

The angora rabbit's long fur is used to make clothing.

Cottontail rabbit

Cottontail rabbits are found in North, South and Central America. They are called cottontails because their tails look like small balls of cotton.

RABBIT FACTS

Rabbits are crepuscular. This means that they come out around sunrise and sunset, in the early morning and early evening.

Rabbits eating at **dawn**

A rabbit's front teeth never stop growing. They need to eat lots of grass and **gnaw** on sticks to keep their teeth from growing too long.

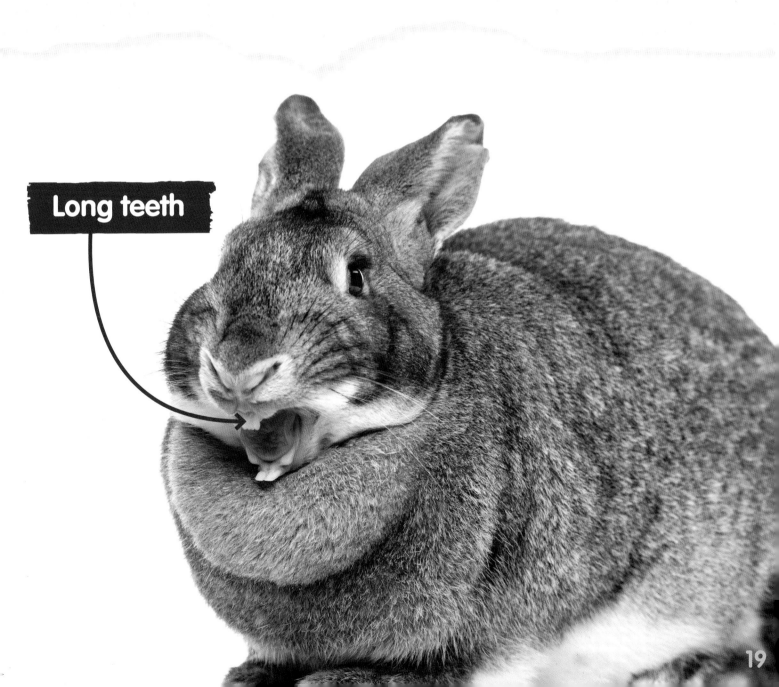

Long teeth

WORLD RECORD BREAKERS

Longest Ears on a Rabbit

The longest ears measured on a lop-eared rabbit were 79 centimetres! Lop-eared rabbits usually have ears that are 50 centimetres long.

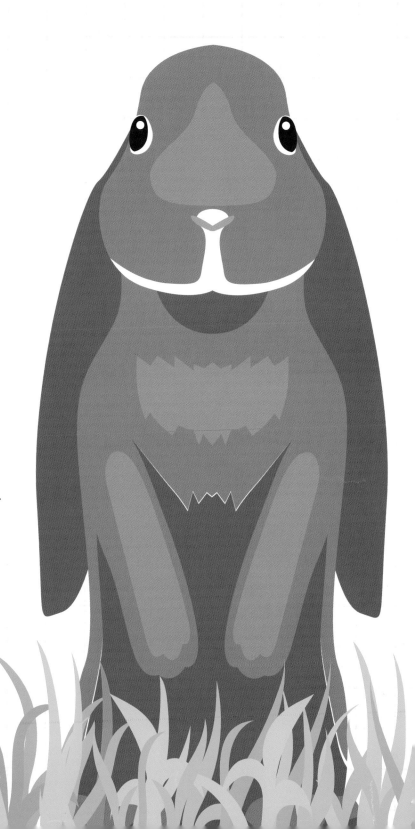

Most Slam Dunks in One Minute

Bini the rabbit can play basketball! In one minute, Bini put a small basketball through a hoop seven times!

LIFE CYCLE OF A RABBIT

1 A doe gives birth to a litter of kittens.

2 The kittens begin to see, hear and grow fur.

LIFE CYCLES

4 The adult rabbits make their own burrows to have their own kittens in.

3 The kittens leave the burrow and start to eat grass.

GET EXPLORING!

Visit a farm or a petting zoo to learn more about rabbits.

Have you ever seen a rabbit in your local area? Do you have a pet rabbit at home? Do any of your friends?

GLOSSARY

breeds	groups of animals in the same species that have similar features
burrows	holes or tunnels dug by an animal and used as a home
dawn	the first daylight that appears in the morning
gnaw	to chew an object again and again
herbivores	animals that only eat plants
mammal	an animal that has warm blood, a backbone and produces milk
mate	a partner (of the same species) that an animal chooses to produce young with
predators	animals that hunt other animals for food
pregnant	when a mother develops a baby inside her
species	a group of very similar animals or plants that are capable of producing young together
weaned	when young stop drinking their mother's milk

INDEX

PHOTO CREDITS

All images are courtesy of Shutterstock.com, unless otherwise specified. With thanks to Getty Images, Thinkstock Photo and iStockphoto. Front cover – JIANG HONGYAN. 1 – JIANG HONGYAN. 2 – Grigorita Ko. 3 – Roselynne, Anupong Thiprot, yevgeniy11. 4 – LovArt, Rawpixel.com, Kang Sunghee, Hans Kim. 5 – Pentium5. 6 – SUPACHAI TAISAENG. 7 – Olha Sem. 8 – HHsu. 9 – tawan. 10 – Cora Mueller. 11 – William Booth. 12 – Nick Biemans. 13 – MestoSveta. 14 – Stefan Rotter. 15 – Naveen Macro. 16 – Grigorita Ko. 17 – Abdecoral. 18 – HongtaeStocker. 19 – Eric Isselee. 20 – Maquiladora, robuart, Valerii_M. 21 – Sudowoodo. 22 – Monika Surzin, Nick Biemans, Roselynne, Rosa Jay. 23 – BestPhotoPlus.